The Maine Menu

Simple recipes for easy living

Meagan Dobson
Sherrill Osgood

Copyright © 2021 Meagan Dobson And Sherrill Osgood.

All rights reserved. No part of this publication may be reproduced, distributed, or transmitted in any form or by any means, including photocopying, recording, or other electronic or mechanical methods, without the prior written permission of the publisher, except in the case of brief quotations embodied in critical reviews and certain other noncommercial uses permitted by copyright law.

CONTENTS

Foreword 1

Brilliant Breakfasts

Awful Waffles... 5
Canoe Cranberry Bread.................................. 7
Simple Smoothie.. 9
Pastrami and Spinach Quiche.......................11
Pie Crust 13

Lovely Lunches

Pan-Fried Burgers 17
Chipotle Sausage Sandwiches...................... 19
Dilly Tuna Melts 21
Bangor BLTs.. 23
Friendly Crab Cakes.....................................25
Heavenly Vegetable Tart 27
Puff pastry 29
Fish House Haddock 31
Lucky Lobster Rolls...................................... 33
Fresh Vegetable Pasta.................................. 35
Tyler's Fish Reuben......................................37
Wicked Cheese Board................................... 39

CONTENTS

Delightful Dinners

Pemaquid Chowder..43
Bacon Fat Pork Chops...45
Damariscotta Dinner Omelet...47
Northeast Quesadilla 49
Salty Sausage Pizza 51
Pizza Crust...53
Sherrill's Beef Stew..55
Meg's Maine Shrimp Sauté 57
Parmesan Baked Chicken 59
Traditional Fried Clams 61
Sautéed Paprika Chicken 63
Ham and Sweet Potato Suppah' 65
Best Beef Curry 67
Paula's Enchiladas 69

Delicious Desserts

Becky's Blueberry Pie..73
Elsie's Peach Cobbler..75
Cinnamon Whoopie Pies...77

FOREWORD

When a series of events brought grandmother and granddaughter together under one roof, it was time to put each other to the test in the kitchen. Two generations sharing space, sharing memories, sharing recipes and sharing the dinner table. Life is a mystery, and you never know what challenges arise. But one thing is consistent: The dinner table is always a place where laughs and smiles can be shared. This is a cookbook written in Maine by two generations of women in the same family. Each recipe is inspired by simple cooking. The recipes are easy and can be prepared for two or more people. From Simple Smoothies to Friendly Crab Cakes. This cookbook is perfect for your Maine adventure. We hope you enjoy it.

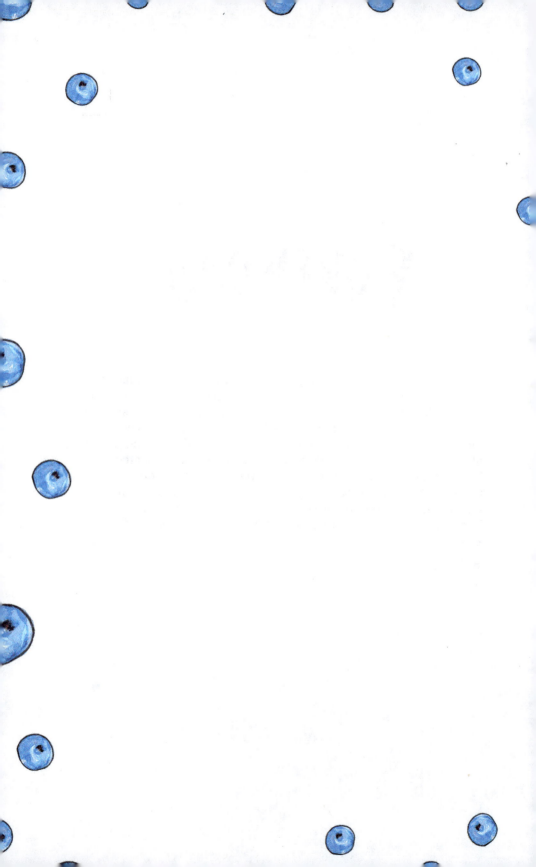

Brilliant Breakfasts

Awful Waffles

Total: 25 minutes
Equipment: Waffle Iron

Ingredients

1 ⅓ cups all-purpose flour

3 teaspoons baking powder

½ teaspoon salt

2 egg yolks, beaten

1 cup milk

¼ cup oil or melted shortening

2 egg whites, beaten until stiff

6 tablespoons unsalted butter

Real Maine syrup

Directions

1. In a large bowl, sift together flour, baking powder and salt. Then, in a separate bowl combine beaten egg yolks, milk, and oil. Stir into dry ingredients. Lastly, fold in beaten egg whites in the mixture

2. Pour mixture into waffle iron. Press cover down. Cook for 3 minutes. Open cover. Serve with real Maine syrup. Enjoy.

CANOE CRANBERRY BREAD

Total: 1 hour

Ingredients

2 cups flour

¾ cups sugar

1 ½ teaspoons baking powder

1 teaspoon salt

½ teaspoon baking soda

¾ cup orange Juice

2 tablespoons vegetable oil

1 tablespoon orange peel zest (grated)

1 egg (beaten)

1 ½ cups chopped cranberries (fresh or frozen)

Nonstick cooking spray, parchment paper or butter

Directions

1. Preheat oven to 350°F. Spray a 9-by-5-inch loaf pan with nonstick cooking spray, line with parchment paper or rub inside with butter.

2. In a medium bowl, mix together flour, sugar, baking powder, salt and baking soda. Slowly stir in orange juice to prevent clumps. Add vegetable oil, grated orange peel and egg. Mix together until smooth. Then, fold in the cranberries.

3. Pour batter into the prepared pan. Bake for 45 minutes or until the top is golden brown and an inserted toothpick comes out clean.

SIMPLE SMOOTHIE

Total: 5 minutes

Ingredients

½ cup vanilla yogurt

1 tablespoon nut butter (e.g., peanut butter or almond butter)

½ cup fresh Maine wild blueberries

½ cup fresh pineapples

1 cup spinach

¾ cup orange juice

2 tablespoons Maine honey

Directions

1. Add all of the ingredients into a blender and blend until smooth. Serve immediately and enjoy.

PASTRAMI AND SPINACH QUICHE

Total: 1 hour

Ingredients

One freshly baked pie crust (pg. 13)

½ cup sliced onion (sweet or Vidalia)

¾ cup chopped pastrami

1 cup shredded Swiss cheese

1 ¼ cups half-and-half

3 large eggs

1 tablespoon fresh garlic, chopped

½ cup chopped spinach

Salt and pepper to taste

Directions

1. Once pie dough has chilled, place it on a lightly flour dusted countertop. Using a rolling pin, gently roll the dough from the center to the edge. Periodically, lift the dough gently and rotate it.

2. Position the dough over your pie pan, easing it into the pan. Trim the edges as necessary and flute as desired.

3. Place the piecrust in a preheated oven at 350°F, and bake for 10 to 15 minutes until crust is semi-baked.

4. Once crust has finished baking, begin adding the filling. First, add a layer of onions. Then, combine pastrami and Swiss cheese and sprinkle them over the onion layer.

5. In a medium bowl, whisk together eggs, half-and-half, garlic, spinach, salt and pepper. Pour this filling on top of the onion, pastrami and Swiss cheese layer. Bake at 350°F until set, about 35 to 50 minutes. Allow to cool for 30 minutes before serving.

PIE CRUST

Total: 1 hour

Ingredients

2 ½ cups all-purpose flour

½ tablespoon sugar

½ teaspoon salt

½ pound unsalted butter

7 tablespoons cold water

Directions

1. Place the flour, salt and sugar designated for the crust into a bowl. Mix the ingredients with a wooden spoon until they are fully integrated.

2. Dice cold butter and add into the mixture. Stir until coarse crumbs form.

3. Add ice water and mix until small beads have begun to form. Press one of the beads between your fingers to test if it has enough water. If the dough sticks together, it has enough. If not, add another teaspoon of water one at a time until it does.

4. Dust a countertop with flour and transfer dough onto it. The dough should be smooth. Do not knead dough. Flatten dough with hands to form two disks each the size of your pie pan, and then cover them with plastic wrap. Refrigerate the dough for one hour before moving on to the next step.

Note: When baking pie crust, poke holes in the bottom and sides of the crust using a fork to prevent the dough from rising.

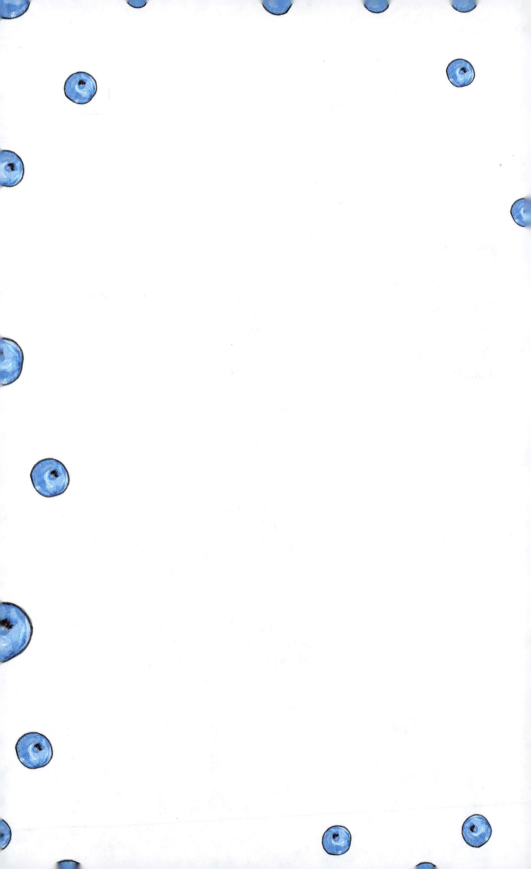

Lovely Lunches

PAN-FRIED BURGERS

Total: 25 minutes

Ingredients

Burgers:

1 pound ground beef (85/15 works best)

1 tablespoon olive or avocado oil

1 tablespoon Dijon mustard

Sea salt

Fresh black pepper

4 ounces raw Cheddar (shredded or sliced)

8 tomato slices

Several large iceberg lettuce leaves for wrapping

Sauce:

¼ cup mayonnaise

2 tablespoons ketchup

½ teaspoon yellow mustard

½ teaspoon apple cider vinegar

1 tablespoon pickle relish

Directions

1. Start with sauce. Mix all sauce ingredients together until fully integrated, then place in the refrigerator.

2. In a medium bowl, mix together beef, oil, Dijon mustard, salt and pepper. Then, lightly form beef mixture into four patties.

3. Place 1 to 2 patties at a time in a medium pre-heated pan, and cook for 3 to 4 minutes on each side. Wait until burgers are cooked thoroughly. Add cheese, cover pan and allow cheese to melt.

4. Finish by removing the cooked burgers from the pan and adding a dollop of sauce to the burger. Then, add tomatoes, wrap in lettuce and enjoy.

Chipotle Sausage Sandwiches

Total: 15 minutes

Ingredients

¼ cup mayonnaise

1 teaspoon paprika powder

1 teaspoon chili powder

1 teaspoon garlic powder

1 teaspoon cayenne powder

½ teaspoon cumin

A healthy pinch of salt and pepper

¼ pound spicy sausage

4 slices ciabatta bread

Directions

1. In a medium bowl, combine mayonnaise, paprika, chili powder, garlic powder, cayenne powder, cumin, salt and pepper. Mix well to form chipotle sauce.

2. Remove spicy sausage from the package, and slice off the needed amount. The remainder can be stored in a food storage container until ready to use. Slice sausage into small, quarter-inch thick pieces, and cook in a skillet over medium heat. While doing this, set the oven to broil and toast the inside of the ciabatta bread slices.

3. Once sausage is cooked, place the desired amount of sausage on two of the baked bread pieces. On the other two, smear a helping of chipotle sauce. Put them together to form two sandwiches.

DILLY TUNA MELTS

Total: 10 minutes

Ingredients

1 can Albacore tuna

2 tablespoons mayonnaise

Salt and pepper to taste

1 teaspoon balsamic vinegar

2 slices multigrain bread

1 teaspoon fresh dill

2 slices Havarti cheese

2 slices tomato

Dill pickle (for serving)

Directions

1. In a small bowl, combine tuna, mayonnaise, vinegar and fresh dill. Pile tuna onto one of the bread slices. Top the other slice with Havarti cheese and sliced tomato.

2. Place bread slices into the oven. Broil lightly for about 5 minutes until cheese is melted and the tuna is heated throughout.

3. Remove them from the oven. Place one slice on top of the other and cut in half. Serve with a quarter sliced dill pickle on the side and enjoy.

BANGOR BLTs

Total: 12 minutes

Ingredients

4 bacon slices

2 leaves romaine lettuce

1 thick tomato slice

2 slices whole-grain bread, toasted in oven

1 tablespoon mayonnaise

Dill pickle (for serving)

Directions

1. Cook bacon in a cast iron skillet over medium-high heat until crispy. Remove the excess oil from bacon by allowing them to rest on a paper towel-lined plate.

2. Add mayonnaise to one slice of toasted bread and layer the bacon, lettuce and tomato on the other slice. Bring the two sides together, cut in half and serve with a dill pickle wedge.

FRIENDLY CRAB CAKES

Total: 30 minutes

Ingredients

1 large egg, beaten

⅓ cup mayonnaise

2 tablespoons Dijon mustard

2 teaspoon Worcestershire sauce

½ teaspoon hot sauce

Salt and pepper to taste

1 pound fresh Maine crab meat

¾ cup Panko bread crumbs

2 tablespoons fresh parsley

3 tablespoons of olive oil

Tartar sauce (For serving)

Lemon wedges (Optional for serving)

Directions

1. Using a small bowl combine: egg, mustard, Worcestershire sauce, hot sauce, salt and pepper. Whisk them together until well mixed.

2. In a separate bowl, stir together crab meat, bread crumbs and parsley. Gently fold in mayonnaise and sculpt into eight patties.

3. Using a large skillet over medium-high heat, heat olive oil until a droplet of water immediately sizzles on impact. Add crab cakes and cook (in batches of two or three) until golden brown on both sides. About 2 minutes per side.

(OPTIONAL)

4. Serve with tartar sauce and lemon wedges.

HEAVENLY VEGETABLE TART

Total: 30 minutes

Ingredients

1 cup shredded Mozzarella cheese (Optional)

1 large egg

2 tablespoons grated parmesan

1 teaspoon chopped rosemary

1 finely grated garlic clove

¾ cup Ricotta cheese

All-purpose flour (to prevent the pastry from sticking)

14 ounces of homemade puff pastry (pg. 29)

Salt and pepper to taste

Various sliced vegetables (tomatoes, zucchini and onions are recommended)

Extra virgin olive oil

Microgreens for serving

Directions

1. Slide rack to the center of the oven and preheat to 425°F. Line a baking sheet with parchment paper.

2. In a medium bowl, combine egg, parmesan, rosemary, garlic, salt and pepper. Beat in Ricotta until the mixture becomes smooth.

3. On a flat and lightly floured surface, roll out puff pastry until it is about 1/8-inch thick. Move the dough onto a lined baking sheet. Using a knife, score a ¾-inch thick border without cutting the pastry all the way through. Then, prick the border with a fork all the way around.

4. Spread Ricotta mixture on top of dough, making sure to keep within the border. Add vegetables on top. Sprinkle some olive oil, salt and pepper on the top and then bake.

5. Once the tart is lightly golden (around 25 minutes), transfer it onto a cooling rack and allow it to cool before eating. Serve with raw microgreens on top.

PUFF PASTRY

Total: 2 hours

Ingredients

1 cup all-purpose flour

¼ teaspoon fine salt

5 ounces of unsalted butter, cold, cut into ¼ inch cubes

⅓ cup ice cold water

Directions

1. In a medium bowl, add the flour and salt. Stir to mix. Add cubed butter. Using a pastry blender or two knives, cut the butter into the dough. When it resembles coarse cornmeal it will be finished. The butter should be in uniform pieces, all about the size of peas.

2. Make a hole in the center of the dough. Add water. Using a rubber spatula or your fingers, stir to combine the dough.

DO NOT KNEAD. The dough will be sticky.

3. Flour a cutting board, and add the dough. Knead a few times by hand and gather the dough into a ball. Wrap in plastic wrap. Allow the dough to chill overnight or for 40 minutes in the freezer.

4. On a lightly floured board roll the dough into a rectangle about 12 inches long. Lift and rotate the dough to prevent sticking.

5. Fold the dough in thirds. Rotate the dough 90 degrees and repeat. Use flour as needed to prevent dough from sticking.

6. Cover with plastic wrap and chill for at least 30 minutes. Repeat the rolling and folding of the dough about 5 or 6 times. Allow the dough to rest between two turns.

7. Cover the dough completely and chill overnight.

Fish House Haddock

Total: 25 minutes

Ingredients

2 Maine Haddock filets

3 cloves of minced garlic

⅓ cup white wine

2 tablespoons melted butter

2 tablespoons lemon juice

1 tablespoon capers

Salt and pepper to taste

2 teaspoon dried dill or 2 sprigs fresh dill

Directions

1. Preheat oven to 375°F and arrange Maine Haddock filets on a baking sheet with enough space for ingredients set aside.

2. In a medium mixing bowl, combine garlic, white wine, melted butter, lemon juice, capers, salt, and pepper.

3. Pour mixture over Haddock filets, spooning it over top of the filets a few times to ensure an even coating. Sprinkle 1 teaspoon of dill onto the top of each filet, or arrange dill sprigs on top.

4. Bake at 375°F for 15 to 20 minutes or until flaky. Serve with a drizzle of sauce from pan.

Lucky Lobster Rolls

Total: 20 minutes

Ingredients

1 ½ pounds cooked lobster meat cut into ¾-inch pieces

¼ cup mayonnaise

2 tablespoons lemon juice

¼ cup celery, chopped

1 tablespoon chives, minced

Salt and pepper to taste

4 hotdog buns (Sourdough if available)

2 tablespoons softened butter

Potato chips (for serving)

Lemon wedges

Directions

1. In a large bowl, combine lobster, mayonnaise, lemon juice, celery, chives, salt and pepper. Stir gently to not break up the lobster meat any further.

2. Spread the butter evenly over the outside of each hotdog bun. Place buns in a pan and sear over medium heat until golden brown (2 to 3 minutes per side).

3. Divide lobster mixture into the buns and serve with a lemon wedge and potato chips.

FRESH VEGETABLE PASTA

Total: 35 minutes

Ingredients

8 oz uncooked linguine

1 cup sliced fresh carrots

2 cups sliced cherry tomatoes

1 cup fresh broccoli florets

1 cup chopped green pepper

1 cup thin-sliced yellow squash

½ teaspoon minced garlic

1 tablespoon olive oil

1 tablespoon fresh minced basil

1 teaspoon fresh minced oregano

1 teaspoon fresh minced thyme

Fresh grated parmesan cheese

Salt and pepper to taste

Directions

1. In a medium pot, add salt and water. Bring to a rolling boil. Add in pasta and cook until slightly tender. Stir pasta occasionally to ensure it doesn't stick to the bottom of the pot.

2. While pasta cooks, in a large, non-stick pan sauté carrots in olive oil until tender.

3. Once carrots are tender and can be easily pierced with a fork, add garlic and cook for 1 additional minute. Then, stir in the remaining ingredients (except for the pasta). Bring to a boil, then reduce heat and let simmer for 8 to 10 minutes uncovered.

4. As pasta finishes, let it drain and set it to the side.

5. Once vegetables have finished simmering, remove them from the heat and stir in the pasta.

6. Sprinkle with fresh parmesan cheese and serve.

Tyler's Fish Reuben

Total: 25 minutes

Ingredients

½ cup milk

½ cup plain bread crumbs

4 (5-oz.) Maine haddock fish filets

3 tablespoons oil

2 tablespoons butter

8 slices pumpernickel bread

4 slices Swiss cheese

¾ cup sauerkraut

½ cup Thousand Island dressing

Directions

1. Place milk in a bowl and bread crumbs on a plate. Then, dip haddock filets into the milk. Then, gently dip the filets into the bread crumbs until lightly covered.

2. Heat oil in a large skillet over medium-high heat. Add fish and cook 6 to 10 minutes or until fish flakes easily with a fork; turning once. Remove fish from skillet and place on a plate. Discard oil.

3. Spread butter on each slice of bread. Then, place four of the slices, buttered side down, on a work surface. Top each with a cheese slice and fish fillet. Then, add sauerkraut and spicy tartar dressing. Cover with remaining slices of bread, keeping the butter on the outside.

4. Heat skillet over medium-low heat until hot. Add sandwiches and cook until the bread has browned and cheese is melted. Enjoy.

WICKED CHEESE BOARD

Total: 10 minutes

Ingredients

Wooden tray, cutting board, or baking sheet for assembling

⅛ of a wheel of aged Cheddar cheese

⅛ of a wheel of Camembert cheese

⅛ of a wheel of Edam cheese

Several slices prosciutto, salami and mortadella

1 cup green olives with pimento

¼ cup cashews

½ cup dried cranberries

½ bar dark chocolate

Half loaf of French bread, cut into slices

Some grapes, still on the vine

A few sprigs of fresh rosemary

Directions

1. Arrange the various ingredients on a wooden tray, cutting board or baking sheet and serve at a party. The ingredients may be interchanged as well to fit your preference.

DELIGHTFUL DINNERS

PEMAQUID CHOWDER

Total: 45 minutes

Ingredients

4 tablespoons unsalted butter

1 sweet Vidalia onion, chopped

4 cups water

2 Maine-grown potatoes, cubed

About 1 to 1 ½ lbs. of skinned, fresh Maine haddock cut into chunks

1 lb. fresh Maine scallops, quartered

1 lb. fresh Maine shrimp

2 cups of heavy Cream

Salt to taste

White pepper to taste

¼ teaspoon dried dill

Directions

1. Using a 5 to 7-quart pot over medium heat, combine dill and butter. Once melted, add onion and stir frequently to avoid sticking. Cook until onion becomes translucent. Set aside.

2. In a 3 to 4-quart pot, add water and potatoes. Boil until tender, about 10 minutes. Remove the potatoes with a slotted spoon and add them to the butter and onion pot. Stir in the potato water as well and return to medium-low heat.

3. Add the haddock, shrimp and scallops to the mixture. Cook until the fish flakes easily with a fork, the shrimp become pink and the scallops are opaque.

4. Slowly stir in heavy cream, salt and pepper. Simmer gently over low-heat for at least fifteen minutes. For a thicker stew, simmer for longer.

5. Serve hot with oyster crackers or saltines and enjoy.

BACON FAT PORK CHOPS

Total: 25 minutes

Ingredients

4 bone-in pork chops

1 tablespoon Dijon mustard

1 teaspoon garlic powder

1 teaspoon onion powder

Salt and pepper to taste

1/2 teaspoon cayenne pepper

4 bacon strips

1/2 cup olive oil

1/2 cup all-purpose flour

Directions

1. Using a small bowl, combine garlic powder, onion powder and cayenne pepper.

2. Pat dry pork chops with a cloth or paper towel. Then, rub Dijon mustard on the pork chops and begin sprinkling the spice mixture onto both sides, rubbing it in. Finish by dipping both sides of each pork chop in flour and setting them aside.

3. Fry bacon strips over medium-high heat until they are crisp, and the fat has drained into the pan.

4. Add olive oil to the pan over medium heat, and allow the oils to mix and warm to cooking temperature.

5. Dredge each pork chop in flour again, and then place each piece in the frying pan. Each side will require about 4 to 5 minutes to become crispy golden brown and for the internal temperature to reach medium. Use a small utensil to check inside of the pork chops to ensure they are completely cooked through with a very pale pink or white coloring.

6. Remove the pork chops from the heat and allow to rest for a few minutes before serving with a side of bacon.

DAMARISCOTTA DINNER OMELET

Total: 20 minutes

Ingredients

4 large eggs

¼ cup whole milk

salt and pepper to taste

1 tablespoon butter

½ cup fresh Damariscotta oyster creek mushrooms

½ cup diced tomato

3 tablespoons minced green onion

½ cup shredded Havarti cheese

Directions

1. Combine eggs, salt, pepper and milk in a bowl and beat until well mixed.

2. Add butter to a medium nonstick skillet and place over medium-high heat. Once the butter is melted, add the egg mix.

3. As the eggs heat up and solidify, pull the cooked portions to the center and allow the uncooked egg to flow underneath so eggs cook evenly. Continue to cook until the bottom is lightly golden and the top is still moist.

4. Add mushrooms, tomatoes, green onions and cheese to the top of the omelet. Then, fold the omelet in half and cook for one minute longer until the cheese has fully melted. Cut in half and enjoy.

NORTHEAST QUESADILLA

Total: 20 minutes

Ingredients

1 tablespoon extra-virgin olive oil

2 bell peppers, sliced into strips

½ Vidalia onion

Salt and pepper to taste

1 pound chicken breasts, sliced into strips

4 flour tortillas

2 cups shredded Monterey Jack cheese

2 cups shredded Cheddar cheese

2 tablespoon vegetable oil

2 minced chives

1 cup sour cream (optional)

½ teaspoon chili powder

½ teaspoon ground cumin

½ teaspoon oregano

Directions

1. Heat olive oil in a skillet. Add peppers, onions, salt and pepper. Cook until the peppers are soft and the onions are slightly transparent.

2. In a frying pan heat 1 tablespoon vegetable oil over medium-high heat. Toss in chicken breast, along with the remaining seasonings. Cook until the chicken breast has a golden outside and is cooked through. Transfer chicken breast onto a plate.

3. In a large skillet over medium heat, add the remaining vegetable oil Add a single soft flour tortilla. Top half of it with chicken mixture, vegetable mixture and a healthy dose of both cheeses. Add chives on top. Then, fold the tortilla over to form a half circle and cook. Flip once. It's finished when both sides are golden and the cheese is fully melted. Repeat this process to make the remaining three quesadillas.

4. Serve whole or as slices, and top with sour cream.

Salty Sausage Pizza

Total: 20 minutes

Ingredients

1 16-ounce package sausage (hot, mild or sweet depending on preference)

Fresh homemade pizza crust (pg. 53)

1 ½ cups of pizza sauce

2 ½ cups of shredded Italian blend cheese

1 Bell pepper diced

Directions

1. Preheat oven to 425°F.

2. On a lightly floured surface, roll the pizza dough into one round, flatten with your hands, pushing from center of the dough outward. Gently stretch the dough until it reaches the desired diameter. Allow to rest for 5 minutes.

3. Place the stretched dough on a greased pizza pan or flat baking sheet. Cover in ¾ cups sauce and 1 cup cheese. Add sausage pinched into one-inch pieces onto the pizza. Sprinkle with green pepper and the remaining cheese.

4. Bake at 400 F (200C) until crust is golden brown and sausage is cooked through (10 to 15 minutes)..

Pizza Crust

Total: 40 minutes
Yield: 1 large or 2 small pizzas

Ingredients

4 tablespoon warm water

1 tablespoon Active Dry Yeast

2 cups bread flour

1 cup cool water

1 teaspoon salt

1 ounce olive oil

1 tablespoon honey

Directions

1. Stir the yeast into the warm water to dissolve. Add flour.

2. Stir the cool water, salt, olive oil and honey into the flour mixture. Knead on low to medium speed with a dough hook or by hand until smooth and elastic, approximately 5 minutes

3. Place the dough in a highly greased bowl and cover. Allow the dough to rise in a warm place for 30 minutes.

4. Punch down the dough and divide into portions. The dough may be wrapped and refrigerated for up to two weeks.

Sherrill's Beef Stew

Total: 3 hours

Ingredients

1 pound stew beef, cut into cubes

¼ cup all-purpose flour

Salt and pepper to taste

3 whole sliced carrots

1 cup sliced parsnips

2 medium potatoes, cut into small chunks

¼ cup radishes (optional)

1 whole sliced white onion

1 can whole kernel corn (not drained)

3 cups beef broth

Directions

1. Add stew beef to a large frying pan over medium heat. Sprinkle it with flour and salt and cook until brown. Then, remove from heat.

2. In a pot, add cooked stew beef, carrots, parsnips, potatoes, radishes, can of corn and beef broth. Cover pot and cook over low heat for 3 hours. Add salt and pepper to taste, and enjoy.

MEG'S MAINE SHRIMP SAUTÉ

Total: 20 minutes

Ingredients

1 pound uncooked Maine shrimp

8 ounces linguine or spaghetti, depending on preference

4 tablespoons butter

½ pound sliced Maine Mousam Valley mushrooms

1 chopped green pepper

Salt and pepper to taste

½ cup grated Mozzarella cheese

3 cloves of minced garlic

Fresh chopped parsley

Directions

1. Cook pasta according to preference. Al dente is best. Drain and set aside.

2. In a large skillet, heat 2 of the 4 tablespoons of butter over a medium-high heat. Sauté mushrooms and green pepper until soft. Stir in the desired amount of salt and pepper, and set aside.

3. In the same pan, add in shrimp and remaining butter. Sauté over medium-high heat for two minutes. Add in minced garlic and cook until the shrimp become pink and form a C-shape. If they begin to form an O-shape, they're getting overcooked.

4. Stir in mushroom mix and heat through. Serve over pasta and sprinkle with cheese and parsley.

PARMESAN BAKED CHICKEN

Total: 35 minutes

Ingredients

4 boneless, skinless chicken breasts

¾ cup Panko bread crumbs

¼ cup grated parmesan cheese

2 tablespoons melted butter

Salt and pepper to taste

1 cup of marinara sauce

¾ cup Mozzarella cheese

Nonstick cooking spray

Directions

1. Preheat oven to 450°F. Spray baking sheet with nonstick cooking spray.

2. Combine bread crumbs and parmesan cheese in a small bowl. In a separate bowl, add melted butter.

3. Brush butter onto the chicken breast, then dip both sides into the bread crumbs mixture. Repeat with all four breasts. Place them on a baking sheet.

4. Lightly mist the top with a little more oil and bake for about 25 minutes, or until the chicken is cooked through. This may take longer with thicker breasts. Then, remove chicken breast from the oven and spoon 1 tablespoon of marinara over each one, topping it off with Mozzarella cheese.

5. Bake for five more minutes, or until cheese is melted, and serve.

Traditional Fried Clams

Total: 30 minutes

Ingredients

1 pound Maine-sourced shucked clams

1 cup corn flour mix

Salt and pepper to taste

1 cup all-purpose flour

½ teaspoon cayenne pepper

1 cup buttermilk

Oil for frying

Directions

1. Rinse the clams in cold water. Check clams to ensure there are no pieces of shell or grit. Mix dry ingredients together in a bowl. In a separate bowl, submerge clams in buttermilk.

2. Preheat oven to 200°F, and place a baking sheet inside. This will keep all the finished clams warm while the rest are frying. In the meantime, heat enough oil to fry (around 1 quart). This can be done in a sauce pot or deep fryer, whichever is handy.

3. Once the oil is almost to temperature, coat a few clams in the dry mix. Don't do more than can be fried at once, as the clams should go straight from the mix into the fryer.

4. Fry the clams until golden brown, about 2 minutes. Move them onto warming rack in the oven, and repeat until the entire batch is cooked. Serve with a lemon wedge or tartar sauce if desired, and enjoy.

Sautéed Paprika Chicken

Total: 20 minutes

Ingredients

2 boneless, skinless chicken breast halves

1 ½ teaspoon sweet paprika

Salt and pepper to taste

1 ½ tablespoons butter

½ sweet white onion, thinly sliced

⅓ cup white wine

⅓ cup half-and-half cream

Directions

1. Sprinkle chicken on both sides with half of the paprika, salt and pepper.

2. Add 1 tablespoon of butter to a medium nonstick skillet and place over medium-high heat. Once the butter is melted, add the chicken, and sauté until cooked through (about 4 ½ minutes per side). Then, transfer chicken to a plate.

3. Add remaining butter and onion to a skillet. Reduce the heat to a medium temperature and cook covered for 5 minutes. Then, mix in remaining paprika, wine and cream.

4. Boil until the sauce thickens a little, around 2 minutes. Then, return chicken to the skillet and simmer to warm it back up. Season to taste and serve.

HAM AND SWEET POTATO SUPPAH'

Total: 30 minutes

Ingredients

1 ½ pounds sweet potatoes

1 stick butter

Salt and pepper to taste

2 tablespoons brown sugar

½ teaspoon ground cinnamon

1 bone-in ham steak

1 tablespoon yellow mustard

½ teaspoon garlic powder

½ teaspoon onion powder

½ teaspoon black pepper

Directions

1. Boil sweet potatoes in a medium pot until tender enough to cut with a fork. Then, drain.

2. Combine butter, brown sugar and cinnamon, and add it to the drained sweet potatoes. Then, mash sweet potatoes until they are at the desired consistency. Add salt and pepper as desired.

3. Combine garlic powder, onion powder and pepper into a small bowl. Brush yellow mustard on both sides of the ham steak and then rub the dry mix on as well. Add a 1/2-inch water to pan so the meat does not dry while cooking. Sear the steak in a skillet over high heat.

4. Remove ham steak from skillet and place on a platter. Serve with sweet potatoes and enjoy.

BEST BEEF CURRY

Total: 50 minutes

Ingredients

2 pounds beef cut into 2-inch cubes

1 cup chopped sweet white onions

Salt and pepper to taste

2 tablespoons minced garlic

1-2 sprigs of scallions chopped

½ teaspoon cumin

3 medium russet potatoes, quartered

3 ½ heaping tablespoons curry powder

1 ½ tablespoons Garam Masala

3 tablespoons olive oil

Directions

1. Steam beef in pressure cooker for 6 minutes. Strain and set aside.

2. Add oil, onions and garlic to pressure cooker and sauté.

3. In a medium bowl, combine curry powder and Garam Masala and enough water to create a paste. Add this mix to pressure cooker as well, cooking for about three and a half minutes, stirring occasionally.

4. Add beef and salt to the pressure cooker and set stove to high heat. Stir the beef in so that all pieces are evenly coated. Cook until the liquid inside evaporates (1 to 2 minutes).

5. Add boiling water, just to cover meat. Close lid and cook for 5 to 6 minutes.

6. Turn heat off and allow pressure to come down naturally within 20 to 25 minutes. Turn heat on, add potatoes and stir.

7. Once the curry comes to a boil, cover the pressure cooker with a normal pot lid and allow potatoes to cook until tender, about 10 to 15 minutes.

8. Once the potatoes are cooked, add cumin, scallions and stir. Then, turn the heat off and allow the curry to sit for a few minutes before serving. Enjoy.

Paula's Enchiladas

Total: 40 minutes

Ingredients

1 pound lean ground beef

2 cans red enchilada sauce

1 can chopped green chilis

1 package soft flour tortillas

1 ½ cups shredded Cheddar cheese

Nonstick cooking spray or butter

Directions

1. Preheat oven to 375°F, and spray a medium baking dish or pan with cooking spray. Alternatively, take a paper towel and coat the inside with butter.

2. In a medium skillet, brown ground beef over medium-high heat for 5 to 7 minutes, stirring occasionally. Drain the grease and stir in 1/2 cup of the enchilada sauce and chilis.

3. Spread 1/2 cup of the enchilada sauce along the bottom of baking dish. Add about a quarter cup of beef and sauce mixture in the center of each tortilla and sprinkle with the desired amount of cheese. Wrap tortillas tightly and lay them in the baking dish with the seam facing down. Add remaining enchilada sauce on top and sprinkle with the remaining cheese.

4. Bake for 20 to 25 minutes or until the enchilada sauce is steaming and bubbling. Let stand for about 5 minutes, then serve with sour cream. Enjoy with the family.

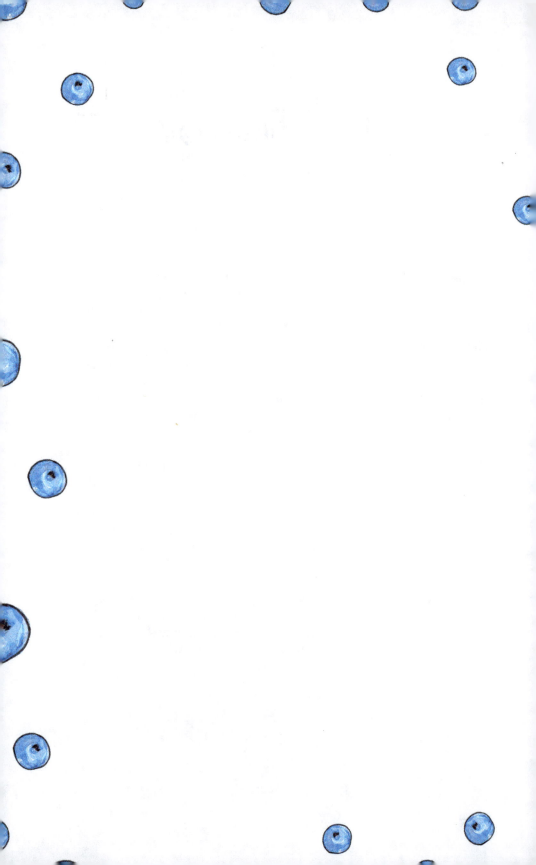

DELICIOUS DESSERTS

Becky's Blueberry Pie

Total: 3.5 hours

Ingredients

One freshly baked pie crust (pg. 13)

5 cups fresh Maine blueberries

¼ cup water

2 tablespoons all-purpose flour

½ cup sugar

⅛ teaspoon salt

Whipped cream for serving, if desired

Directions

1. Place one cup of blueberries into a medium saucepan. Then, in a small bowl, whisk together water and flour and add that to the pan as well. Mix in sugar and salt.

2. Begin cooking on high heat until it first begins to simmer. Then, reduce the heat to medium and stir until the mixture has thickened and the berries have darkened. Remove mixture from the heat and allow it to rest for a few minutes.

3. Using a rubber spatula, fold the remaining blueberries into sauce and mix until everything is well combined. Allow this new mix to sit for a few more minutes before transferring it into the pie crust.

4. Allow the pie to sit at room temperature for 2 to 3 hours before serving. Serve with a dollop of whipped cream, or eat on its own. Enjoy.

Elsie's Peach Cobbler

Total: 45 minutes

Ingredients

4 to 6 cups sliced, ripe Maine peaches

Juice of half a lemon

½ cup white sugar

½ cup light brown sugar

1 cup all-purpose flour

2 teaspoon baking powder

½ teaspoon cinnamon

1 egg

1 teaspoon vanilla extract

½ cup or one stick butter, melted

Vanilla Ice Cream or Whipped Cream for serving

Directions

1. Preheat oven to 375°F. Then, spray a 9-by-13-inch baking dish with nonstick spray or rub it with butter.

2. Spread the peaches out across the bottom of the dish and sprinkle them with lemon juice.

3. In a medium mixing bowl, whisk together sugars, flour, cinnamon and baking powder. In a separate bowl, beat egg, and then add vanilla. Add the mixture to dry ingredients.

4. Mix together until everything is well combined. Then, distribute this mixture over the peaches, and spoon butter over it.

5. Bake for 30 to 35 minutes, and until the top is golden brown and the peaches are bubbling. Allow to cool slightly and serve with preference of ice cream or whipped cream.

Cinnamon Whoopie Pies

Total: 1 hour

Ingredients

For the Cookies:

1 3/4 cups unbleached all-purpose flour

½ teaspoon kosher salt

3/4 cup unsweetened cocoa powder

1 ½ teaspoons baking soda

½ teaspoon baking powder

½ cup (1 stick) unsalted butter, room temperature

1 cup granulated sugar

1 large egg

1 cup buttermilk, room temperature

1 teaspoon pure vanilla extract

For the Cinnamon Filling:

½ cup (1 stick) unsalted butter, room temperature

3 to 4 cups confectioners sugar

Pinch of Kosher salt

Store bought decorative icing

½ teaspoon ground cinnamon

Directions

1. Preheat the oven to 350°F. Line 2 baking pans with parchment paper.

2. In a bowl sift together: flour, salt, cocoa powder, baking soda, and baking powder. Set aside.

3. In a bowl or using a mixer. cream butter and sugar until light and fluffy. Add eggs, buttermilk, and vanilla. Beat until well combined. Add dry ingredients. Mix well.

4. Using a 1-ounce ice cream scoop, drop dough onto prepared baking pan, about 1 inch apart. Bake for 10 to 12 minutes. Remove to a rack to cool.

5. Make the Cinnamon filling: Beat butter on medium speed with an electric mixer until pale, 4 to 5 minutes. Reduce the speed to low and add half the confectioners sugar, beating until just incorporated. Add remaining sugar, cinnamon, and salt and continue beating until fluffy, 1 to 2 minutes.

6. Transfer Cinnamon filling to a pastry bag and snip the end. When cookies have cooled completely, pipe 2 tablespoons filling onto the flat side of half the cookies. Sandwich with remaining cookies, pressing down slightly so that the filling spreads to the edge of the cookies.

7. Use icing to pipe laces on top. Lightly sprinkle cinnamon powder on top of cookies and serve.

NOTES

NOTES

NOTES

NOTES

NOTES

NOTES

NOTES

NOTES

NOTES

NOTES